Belgium …
where angels die …

A disgrace
to the human race

(there is something wrong with this picture)

All characters and events described are fictional … nothing that is told is this story happened … or did it … I don't know (Tara Vanhonacker)

What is Belgium?

With this picture something is wrong and what, that I will tell here … In this book or article which today will be available in two languages for free download …

Who am I ?

My name is Tara and my life is similar to a hell …
In 2011 I gave up on my life in Belgium because my personal situation was hallucinating …
In short, the facts … I was sexually mutilated by my father before I was six months old, I was raped by him when I was 4 years old, I was almost killed by him when I was 11, I was forced by him in jobs and relationships … any financial support he denied me all my life … … between my 35th and 45th he stalked me and bullied in ways that you could call hallucinating …

My mother was weak and self-centered, depressed … she did not intervene and lived in a religious delusional world …
My sister is as much a victim … but her remedy to finish me off … She wants to maintain the good name of my father, while everyone knows that my father was a psychopath and a sociopath …

In 2011 I gave up trying to have any rights in Belgium … visits to lawyers, law centers, police, social workers gave only the bizarre result that I was sent on and on and on … the falsification of my birth certificate does not work in my favor because in Belgium people with a gender variance or hermaphroditism are bullied and thrown out of society … There are laws to protect but it does not work … and in my UNIQUE situation the discrimination beyond belief …
In 2011 I had money and I went to Thailand that I love and where my freedom was not restricted. I am a Buddhist, and that did not help to get help in Belgium, Flanders and I had no family … or rather a dysfunctional family …

In 2012 I left and I have had the misfortune to bump into a criminal situation in Thailand … that is a Thai issue and I mention it only because seven months of my life I spend in a concentration camp in Bangkok, Suang Phlu, just because I refused to return the criminals …
In the book "Angels" you can read what happens inside this hell on Earth.
For readers in Belgium it may seem nothing that around me, people went crazy trying to find a way out, that people died in my arms, that cultural differences lead in this place to deadly fights, that people lost all hope …
I must point out again that I do not blame the Thai government , I just ask them to intervene …

I am a computer science teacher and I spent 25 years teaching at the PCVO Scheldeland in Lokeren.

I'm a writer and artist … and I'm doing astrophysics and quantum physics … I'm unfortunately not stupid ….
And this book shows just what happened … I do not want emotions connected to it … but I can assure you that I almost went crazy from sadness and frustration … for the sake of the

Children of Belgium who are killed by a system that should be history and I shout very hard at the Belgian and Flemish governments to intervene … no human lives must be lost … no more … it's done …

What happened to me when I was back in Belgium ?

How was my health when I arrived ?

My health was bad … I was much too thin and cold like hell … and hungry …
My left leg is hurting, a snake bite has to heal and there is probably something wrong in my foot there and my right hand was at the moment I arrived broken … I was in a lot of pain and had no clothes or shoes …

And then these things happened …

- I arrived in Belgium on 16/02/2016 at 08:00AM … in Brussels airport in Zaventem … the police of Belgian was waiting for me, because I had to be checked for crimes … because the Thai Immigration Act turns a person that gets send away into an International criminal … the check by the Belgian police … showed I had absolutely no criminal record … anywhere in the World … nothing …

- at 08:30 I met a lady from the Red Cross Hasselt who was going to help me a little … she gave some clothes and bought me food and I ate a lot that day … a lot … I told her where I had been, how that prison was and why I had been there … she was nice but professional … and then she took to the City of Ghent in Belgium … something I actually never asked for …

- at 10:00 we went to the CAW Gent and were more or less ordered to go to "De Schelp" … When we tried to talk to the lady in "De Schelp" … she refused to listen and she even shouted at me … that she would never help me …
She phoned the UZ Gent, one of the biggest hospitals in Flanders and finally we went to the Emergency Room of the hospital …

And then all HELL BROKE LOOSE … my life was turned into a physical and mental nightmare …

ONTHAAL

- **algemeen**: CAW-Onthaal
- **jongeren**: JAC / Jongerenonthaal
- **crisis**: De Schelp
- **specifieke groepen:** Transithuis voor personen met een precair verblijfsstatuut, Justitieel Welzijnswerk voor (ex-) gedetineerden en hun directe omgeving, Brugteam voor chronische thuislozen, Slachtofferhulp voor slachtoffers, nabestaanden en naastbestaanden

[[16-02-2016]] [[11:45AM]]

The unthinkable happened ...
I was in the Emergency Room of the hospital with the Lady of the Red Cross and I explained what had happened to me ... briefly ... about Suang Phlu, the hunger, the cold, my broken hand and my left leg and foot ...

I was send to have a bed in a Psychiatric Ward of the hospital ... because someone in Thailand had told the Embassy that I was "crazy" ... and they told the Red Cross ... and they told the hospitals ... no one looked at my hand and the question is and remains why ignore a broken hand ...

Was it because I was homeless in Belgium ?
Was it because my papers that were in the house I rented in That Phanom that were gone?
Was it because I was gender variant ?

There are laws to protect a Belgian citizen from medical malpractice and from the refusal to help a person in need ... maybe they were forgotten ...

I was still in shock ... very much so ...
The person that told everyone I was "crazy", you will find her picture below ... her name is Som Ying Mingkwam from That Phanom in Thailand ...
The person along with Nuchanart Mounmontree who I had told about my Belgian situation ...

Som Ying Mingkwam

[[16-02-2016]] They gave me a bed and a room and I was happy because it was almost a year ago I had slept in a bed ...

I tried to explain to the nursing staff what had happened and the problems I had, but because I had no papers they got nasty ...
I was screened by three very learned psychiatrists and they found absolutely nothing wrong with me ... except for a small problem ... they did not listen when I told them what had happened to me in Thailand ... they refused to listen...
I got told to try to find help from friends, but I was told at first that I could make no phone calls because it cost money ....

I asked the social services of the hospital to make a phone call to Hamme, a city in Belgium, to one person I had cared for ... for more than 15 years ... they said no ...
I had absolutely no money at all ... and I got told "no" ...

And then they threw me out of the hospital and my hand was still broken …

[[20-02-2016]]
I went to the little town I was born in, hoping to see my sister ...
I visited the grave of my mother and paid respect ...
I met a few people and they understood that the closed door of my sisters house, was actually very wrong ... my sister ... does not "lik" someone with a gender variation ... and she does not want to share the little money and properties she has with me ...
This is her house ... and her second house ... and a car ...
and there she works ...

That white house, is the house I grew up in … the room my father raped me is the room upstairs on the right … when I was in Thailand they told me, the house was going to be demolished …

Belgium ... where angels die ... by Tara Vanhonacker ...

In the garden of the house, see below, my father told is he had buried money ... but when he died ... my sister assured me nothing had been found ... and I know she would never ever lie to me ...
she is my sister ...
Where my mother was buried ...

Belgium ... where angels die ... by Tara Vanhonacker ...

(The grave of my mother)

[[20-02-2016]]

No one in Belgium had told me what to do or where to go, so after I went there ... I walked to Gent ... and I went to the police in this police station ...
The officer was nice , but he had a lot of fun with me ... I looked very bad and I was agitated when I tried to tell him that I needed to formulate a complaint against a few people in Thailand ... He started laughing me in the face and directed to another hospital where I went ...

So went to the hospital Jan Palfijn, to the Emergency Room and I told the people there that I had horrible pain in my left leg and foot and that my right hand was broken ... they got me a room in the Pyschiatric ward and again psychiatrists spoke to me ... but nothing was really wrong with me, except that I was suffering from a few things that happened to me in Thailand …

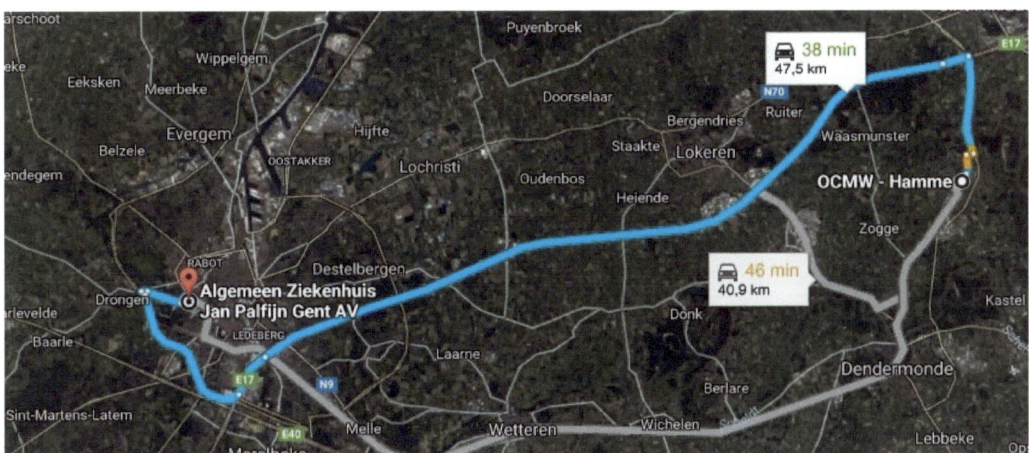

[[21-02-2016]]

I am in the hospital and I feel very bad ... because the pain is not gone ... I tell time and time again that something bad happened to me ... but nothing happens ... and I am being asked to leave ... and they kindly tell me that I need help from the homeless organizations in Ghent, Belgium ...

I ask again that someone call Hamme, that small but nobody wants ...
So the next day I walk ... from Ghent to Hamme, all through the night, because I still do not

know that there actually beds I can sleep in and showers I can take ... I look horrible and the pain is ripping through my body ...

47,5 kilometer in the cold, in the rain and with a broken hand and a left leg that is hurting like hell ... but I walk ... because maybe there is one person a live who wants to help me a little ... here in wonderful Belgium ... after all I was a teacher the school of Hamme for more than 10 years and I know people ...
All through the night ... slowly ... not resting because there is nowhere to sleep ...

[[22-02-2016]]

And I walk and I walk ... between the beautiful houses and in the nice streets of Belgium ... sadly ... I am in the cold outside and I have eaten nothing since yesterday morning ... So try to get closer and closer to Hamme ... OCMW ... maybe they will help me ... And somewhere around 9 AM I get there ... I get received well, I get some food and then they send me back to Ghent, Belgium ... they even refuse to phone my ex-partner and to ask her if she can help me a little …

[[22-02-2016]]

This is where a few homeless people pick me up and start helping me ... Thank you, my friends ...
So here I am a woman, homeless, cold and hungry and I still do not understand what has happened to me ...

Do you think Som Ying Ming Kwam of That Phanom and the family Mounmontree get it ?

[[23-02-2016]]

I am now officially a Belgian homeless person ... but I have no idea what I am supposed to do ... I ask for help but I get ignored and I still do not know nor understand why ...
- because I am gender variant ?
- because I am homeless ?
- because I am a woman ?
- because I am poor ?
- because I am "crazy" ?

I don't know ... these people try to help me ... but is a bit difficult, because I can not explain to them what happened to me in Thailand ... I get the clear message ... I have to shut up about it and let go ... go sit in a corner and beg for money in the streets ...
The PAIN in my hand is inhuman ... and some days I quietly go into a corner and I cry .. and I scream in the streets ... why is no one in Belgium helping me ?
The answer is silence in the wind and I don't know what I am supposed to do ... and then something nasty happens ... very nasty ...
The pictures are from the places where we can sleep between 9PM and 9AM ... and that is only in the wintertime in the summer that starts on march 15 ... there is only place and when your name is high up in the alphabet …

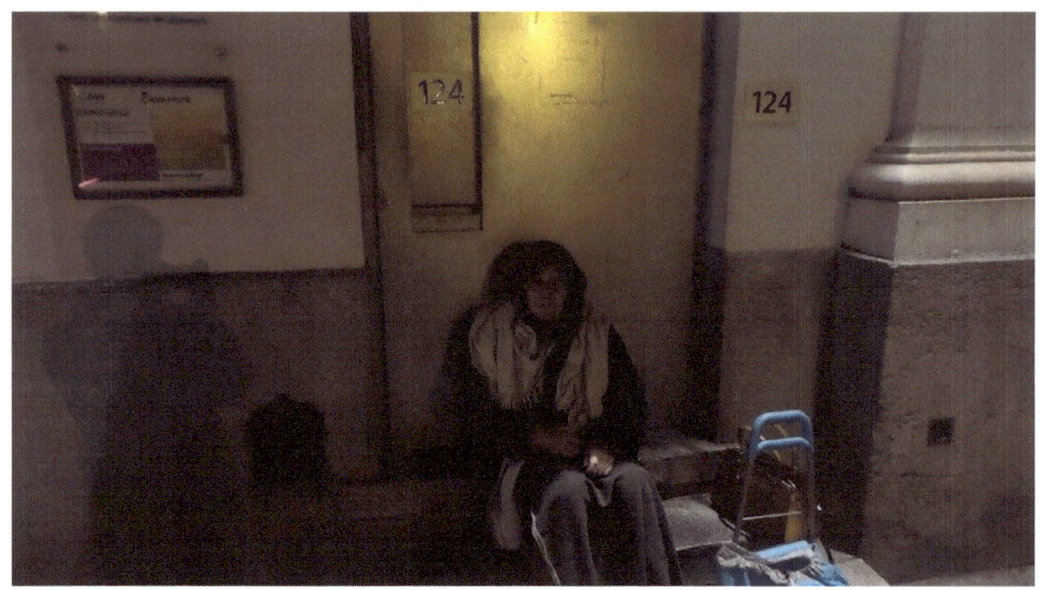

[[05-03-2016]]

If you can not find a place to sleep … you have to sleep here …

[[01-03-2016 == 31-03-2016]]

Every man in Belgium sees my situation and promises a bed and some food in return for sex ... not a relationship ... and if I say no ... I can just die in the streets of Belgium ...
A few of the answers I get from people in Belgium :
- go get a job, when I ask for a stamp so I can find a job
- go get a job, if I want to receive ONE faxmessage
- go get a man, if you want to sleep inside

My hand is no longer broken, the fracture has healed, but in a wrong way ... since yesterday I have an ID - Card for Belgium ... I have a little money I get from the government ... and I have to wait until a solution is found ... but there is no solution in sight ...

The car that was stolen from me
in That Phanom Thailand by Nuchanart Mounmontree

(My house in That Phanom … 2 Moo 6 … 48110 That Phanom Nuea, That Phanom)

(the second house ….)

I have a question to the world ... when are you going to tell the 5 people below what they did to me and when are you going tell them that they have to return the favor ... because I told them ... that Belgium for me is very difficult ... a sao pa phes song ... does not get any help in Belgium ... not any ...
So, my friends in Thailand ...
Does the writer who gave a book to His Majesty the King of Thailand have to suffer and die in Belgium ?
To the Belgium people ...
When a writer gives a book to the head of state of a country ... does that not deserve any respect ... at all ... because this person becomes an ambassador of Belgian culture and values ... because of who SHE is ... the people in Thailand now KNOW what Belgian respect is ...

No wonder I am angry like hell at the Belgian government for punishing me for being the victim of the 5 people below and not supporting me in any way ... but to tell me that my sister got a phone call and promised to help ... and when I was in Belgium ... she even send the police after me, for asking ONE time for her help ... in 20 years ...
There are people in Belgium who have to pay me back loans, and they just refuse to do that ...

BELGIUM ... I still have only one red dress and one black bra ... I do not think you will ever do right by me ... I have been patient ... but I do not want to die ...
The writer who gave a book to His Majesty the King of Thailand ... is being treated very badly ... very badly ... It would the first time that a person who has given an enormous gift to Thailand, dies ... because of 5 people in That Phanom and I think these people can actually be told to change their minds a little and to allow me to go home where my properties are.

Postscriptum :

Can I now please die in peace ... because I do not know what to do anymore ... I keep asking for help, and I get nothing ... except that you listened to me ... I love you very much ... but love is not enough ... it is never enough ...

People want too much ... and they take and keep taking and that is why I want to die ... all hope is gone ... all dreams are gone ... there is nothing anymore but for me to die quickly ...

In the dharma it is said, that you should not hold on to anger ... or it becomes hate and I do not want to hate ...

But sis, I did nothing wrong in my life and when ask people to help me ... they just tell me to "die or go away" ...

When someone comes to me and asks for help ... I don't shout at them ... I don't mock them ... I help them and the only thing I expect back is that they are happy ...

Because me I don't matter to anyone, as far as I can see ...

Please Thai people pray for me and let me die ...

There is no end to my suffering except to die ...

I am not depressed, but the vultures are all around me ... and the pain is beyond belief ...

I break no laws and I do whatever I can to make sure other people are happy ... but the only way I can make Thailand happy is by not being angry at you anymore ...

When a person comes to Thailand , when do you stop taking ? Do you ever show compassion and is there really no one in Thailand who is willing to help me ? Are you so busy making money of foreigners, that you forget that the foreigner sometimes "loves" you ...

Goodbye

I was here and now I am no more ... bye ...

Tara Vanhonacker – August 30 – 2016

www.ingramcontent.com/pod-product-compliance
Lightning Source LLC
Chambersburg PA
CBHW041613180526
45159CB00002BC/831